Kitty Love

Nicola Jane Swinney

QEB

Quarto is the authority on a wide range of topics.

Quarto educates, entertains and enriches the lives of our readers—enthusiasts and lovers of hands-on living.

www.quartoknows.com

© 2018 Quarto Publishing plc

First published in 2018 by QEB Publishing,
an imprint of The Quarto Group.
6 Orchard Road, Suite 100,
Lake Forest, CA 92630, USA
T: +1 949 380 7510
F: +1 949 380 7575
www.QuartoKnows.com

Editor: Harriet Stone
Designer: Melissa Alaverdy

A CIP record for this book is available
from the Library of Congress.

ISBN 978 0 7112 4094 0

Manufactured in Shenzhen, China HH092018

9 8 7 6 5 4 3 2 1

MIX
Paper from
responsible sources
FSC® C017606

The Kitty Love Stats contain information about the color, eye color, and "cuddle factor" of each breed.

Kitty Love Stats

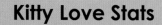

Color	All colors
Eye color	All colors
♥♥♥	✓✓✓✓
★★★	It hasn't forgotten that it was a hunter, but it still loves to play.

Contents

Abyssinian

With its wild beauty, this golden cat is one of our oldest breeds.

Kitty Love Stats

Color	Most shades of gold, plus lilac and silver
Eye color	Gold, copper, green, hazel
🖤🖤	✓✓✓✓
⭐⭐⭐	Its huge ears make it look like the cats worshiped by Ancient Egyptians.

Because these pretty cats are so friendly and playful, they have earned the nickname "Aby-silly-an"! They are sweet and loving, and always want to be close to their human. They are thought to come from what is now Ethiopia in North Africa.

American Bobtail

It looks like a bobtailed wildcat, but this American breed is gentle and loving.

Kitty Love Stats

Color	Black, blue, brown, cream, white
Eye color	All colors
♥♥	✓✓✓✓
★★	Will wag its tail like a dog when happy.

Bobtailed cats have been around for a long time. The American Bobtail is a stocky animal with a big, wedge-shaped head. It is usually a quiet cat but it will trill, chirp, and click when happy.

American Curl

All American Curls can be traced back to a stray black kitten named Shulamith.

Kitty Love Stats

Color	All colors
Eye color	All colors
♥♥♥	✓✓✓✓✓
★★★	Known as the "Peter Pan" of the cat world.

With its backward-curling ears and silky fur, the American Curl is a pretty cat. It makes a great family pet, as it loves children and will follow you around everywhere. American Curls love to play and never really stop being a kitten.

American Shorthair

The first shorthair cats arrived in America with the Pilgrims on the *Mayflower*.

Kitty Love Stats

Color	All colors
Eye color	All colors
♥♥	✓✓✓✓
★★	It hasn't forgotten that it was a hunter, but it still loves to play.

The first shorthairs were very good rat-catchers, but only the fittest cats would have survived the tough journey to America. Shorthairs were prized by farmers because they caught the rats that ate their crops.

Australian Mist

These beautiful cats were bred to be indoor animals, to keep them safe in Australia.

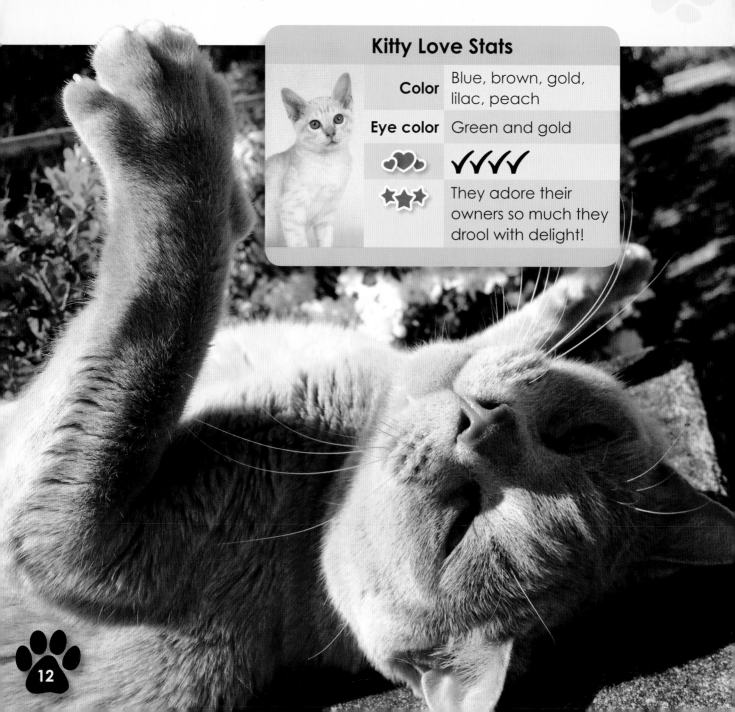

Kitty Love Stats

Color	Blue, brown, gold, lilac, peach
Eye color	Green and gold
♥♥♥	✓✓✓✓
⭐⭐⭐	They adore their owners so much they drool with delight!

Burmese and Abyssinian cats were used to make Australia's only cat breed. Australian Mists are very pretty, with spotted or marbled coats and short, sleek fur. They are playful and loving but can be greedy for food!

Balinese

Elegant and handsome, this is a longhaired type of Siamese, with the same bright blue eyes.

Kitty Love Stats

Color	Seal, blue, tabby, chocolate, lilac, cream, tortoiseshell	
Eye color	Blue	
🤍	✓✓✓✓✓	
⭐	A Balinese loves to sit on your lap!	

Every so often a longhaired Siamese would be born, so two American breeders decided to make a permanent breed of longhaired cats. The two breeders chose the name Balinese after the graceful dancers of Bali.

Bengal

With a stunning coat that is as soft as velvet to the touch, this lovely cat adores affection!

Kitty Love Stats

Color	Various types of tabby, plus seal silver lynx point
Eye color	Green, yellow, gold, blue, aqua
🖤🖤🖤	✓✓✓✓
★★★	A Bengal was once bought for $50,000!

This beautiful breed is the result of crossing a pet cat with an Asian leopard cat. It is the only tame cat with rosette markings, like leopards, jaguars, and ocelots.

Birman

One of the world's favorite cat breeds, the pretty Birman has a lovely nature.

Kitty Love Stats

Color	All colorpoints
Eye color	Blue
♡♡	✓✓✓✓✓
★★★	Like all the pointed breeds, Birman kittens are born pure white.

Like a Siamese, this cat has colored points—a darker face, ears, and tail. Unlike a Siamese, though, its feet are pure white. These striking markings and glowing blue eyes make the Birman one of the most beautiful breeds.

Bombay

This sweet-tempered cat looks like a black panther in miniature!

Kitty Love Stats

Color	Black
Eye color	Gold to copper
♥♥♥	✓✓✓✓✓
★★★	Will sit on your shoulder as you do your chores.

If you want a dog, a cat, and a monkey all rolled into one, you need a Bombay! It is a loving, playful bundle of mischief. The Bombay was bred to look like a black leopard but have a calm and friendly nature.

21

British Shorthair

This cat is round! It has a round body, round eyes, and a round face with a sweet expression.

Kitty Love Stats

Color		Most colors, points, and patterns
Eye color		Blue, orange, or odd-colored eyes
🤍🤍		✓✓✓✓✓
⭐⭐⭐		This cat forms strong bonds with people.

The Romans introduced large numbers of cats to the United Kingdom to catch rats and mice. Those cats bred with wild cats on the islands and the result is today's tame British Shorthair. It is the most popular pedigree cat breed in the UK.

Burmese

This playful breed comes from America, but the original cat, Wong Mau, was from Burma.

Kitty Love Stats

Color	Brown, blue, lilac, red, cream, and tortoiseshell	
Eye color	Green and gold	
🖤🖤	✓✓✓	
⭐⭐⭐	Cats were kept in temples in Burma and even had servants!	

Burmese cats are strong and compact, and their coat is short and glossy. If you like a quiet life, the Burmese probably isn't for you! They are lively, fun-loving cats who love people and want to be involved in everything you do.

Burmilla

The result of an accident, the Burmilla is a very pretty cat with a sweet and open face.

Kitty Love Stats

Color	Silver with black markings
Eye color	Green
🤍🤍	✓✓✓✓✓
⭐⭐	It looks like it is wearing makeup around its eyes.

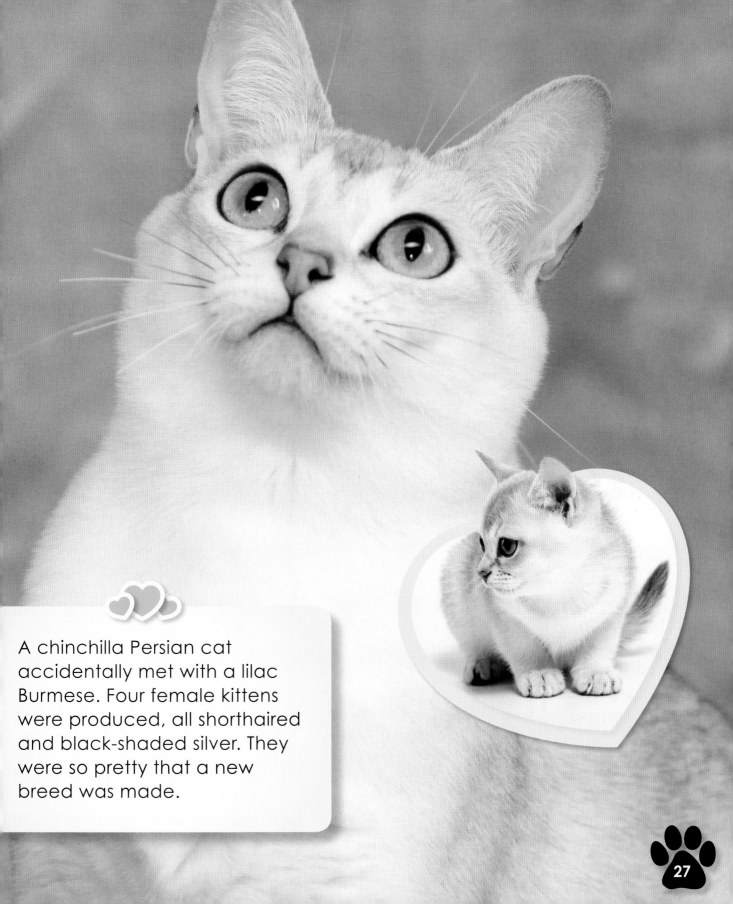

A chinchilla Persian cat accidentally met with a lilac Burmese. Four female kittens were produced, all shorthaired and black-shaded silver. They were so pretty that a new breed was made.

Chartreux

A quiet cat, your Chartreux will chirp at things it finds interesting, instead of meowing.

Kitty Love Stats

Color	Blue
Eye color	Gold to copper
♥♥♥	✓✓✓✓✓
★★★	Its round face and round eyes make it look happy all the time.

This beautiful cat kept French monasteries clear of rats and mice, though the breed probably came from Persia, now called Iran. Rather unkindly, it is sometimes called a "potato on sticks" because it has a solid body on short, slim legs.

Chinese Li Hua

This is a very old breed, but you can't mistake a Chinese Li Hua for any other cat.

Kitty Love Stats

Color	Golden brown with black on the legs and tail
Eye color	Green, yellow, brown
♥♥	✔✔✔
★★★	It is said that cats once ruled China but stopped speaking so they could live an easier life.

Sometimes called the Dragon Li, the Li Hua is a beautiful cat. It has a wide, diamond-shaped head, large almond-shaped eyes, and a short tabby coat that makes it look like a wildcat.

Cornish Rex

An unusual breed, the Cornish Rex never loses its kittenish appeal as it loves to play.

Kitty Love Stats

Color	Solid, silver, shaded
Eye color	Blue, green, gold
♥♥	✓✓✓
★★★	It likes to use its paws to throw and catch objects.

In England in 1950 a cat named Serena had five kittens, one of which had a curly coat. This kitten, named Kallibunker, founded the Cornish Rex breed. The velvet-soft fur forms waves all over the cat's body and feels lovely to touch.

Cymric

This cute and bouncy breed is jokingly said to be the offspring of a cat and a rabbit!

Kitty Love Stats

Color	White, blue, black, red, cream, silver, tortoiseshell, brown
Eye color	Amber, green, gold, hazel, orange, yellow
♡♡	✓✓✓✓✓
⭐⭐⭐	Will act as a "watch cat" and growl at anything out of the ordinary.

Like the Manx cat, the Cymric—pronounced kim-rick—has no tail. Both come from the Isle of Man, off the northwest coast of Great Britain. The Manx has a short coat and Cymric has a long one.

Devon Rex

The curly coat of the Devon Rex is as soft as its personality.

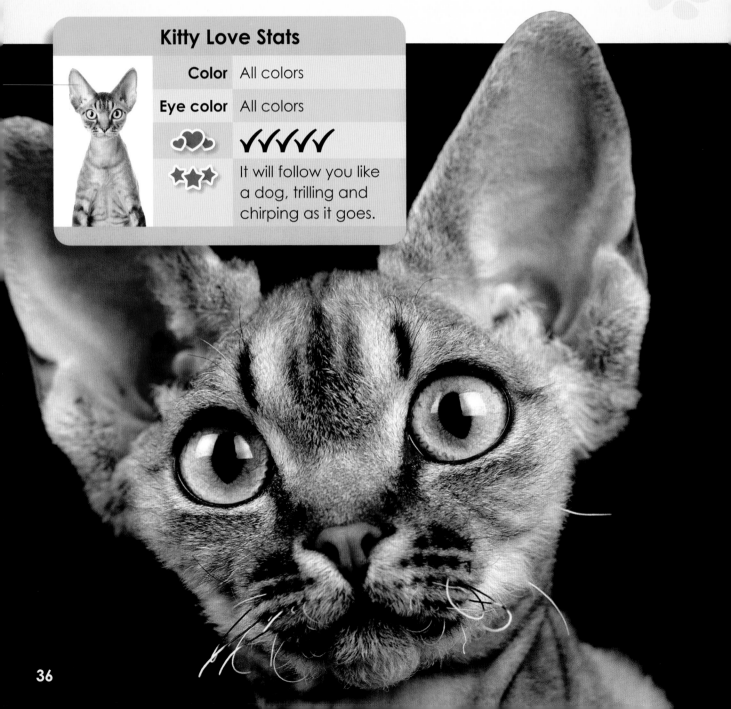

Kitty Love Stats

Color	All colors
Eye color	All colors
🤍🩶	✓✓✓✓✓
⭐⭐⭐	It will follow you like a dog, trilling and chirping as it goes.

This strange-looking breed is sometimes called the pixie of the cat world. It has huge ears set low on its head, a wide face, big eyes, and a long, skinny neck. Though its fur is like that of the Cornish Rex, the two breeds are not related.

Egyptian Mau

Pictures of spotted cats like the Egyptian Mau are shown in art from Ancient Egypt.

Kitty Love Stats

Color	Silver, bronze, smoke
Eye color	Green
♡♡	✓✓✓✓
★★★	The Mau's hind legs are longer than its front legs.

This cat's ancestors belonged to Egyptian pharaohs and kings, adored for their beauty. Maus have mascara-like markings around their slanted eyes, and the legs, tail, chest, and neck are barred—this pattern is sometimes called a "broken necklace."

Exotic Shorthair

This gentle cat is said to be a "Persian in pajamas!" It is pretty and playful.

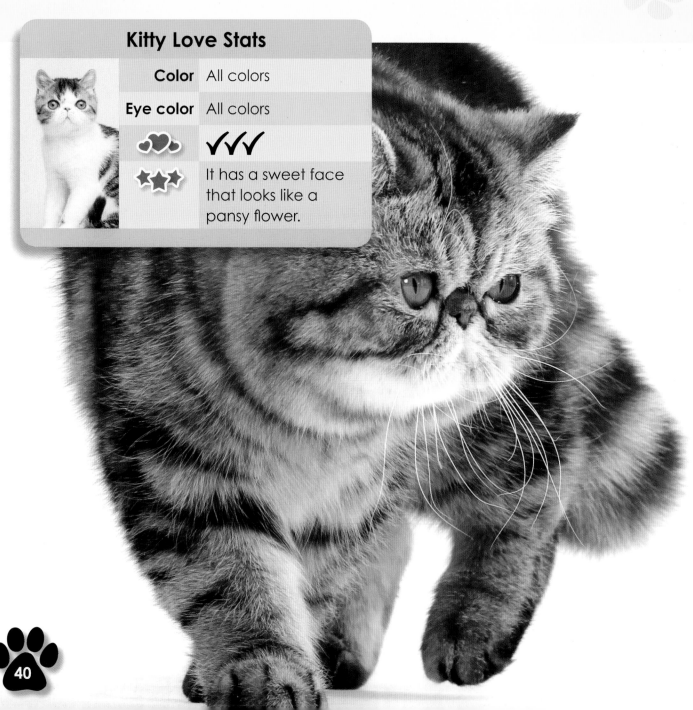

Kitty Love Stats

Color	All colors
Eye color	All colors
🖤🖤	✓✓✓
⭐⭐⭐	It has a sweet face that looks like a pansy flower.

The Exotic Shorthair is bred to be just like the Persian but with a short, dense coat instead of a long, flowing one. It is perfect if you don't want to spend a lot of time grooming your pet cat.

Havana

This cat is a lot heavier to hold than it looks, but it makes a lovely armful!

Kitty Love Stats

Color	Chocolate or lilac brown
Eye color	Green
🖤🖤	✓✓✓✓✓
⭐⭐	The Havana Brown's elegant head is longer than it is wide.

English breeders used Siamese and shorthaired breeds to produce brown-colored cats, whose dark, glossy coats set off their dazzling green eyes. The British Havana looks more oriental than the American version, which is sometimes called the Havana Brown.

Japanese Bobtail

Cats in Japan were used to keep rats and mice away from the rice-paper scrolls in temples.

Kitty Love Stats

Color	All colors, including mi-ke, red, and black on white	
Eye color	All colors, including odd eyes	
♡♡	✓✓✓	
★★	Newborns are quite big and walk earlier than other breeds.	

44

The first tame cats in Japan arrived with Buddhist monks fifteen hundred years ago. As well as guarding the paper scrolls, they were used to protect the silkworms that spun Japan's beautiful silk.

Korat

A very old breed, this unusual cat takes its name from a place in Thailand.

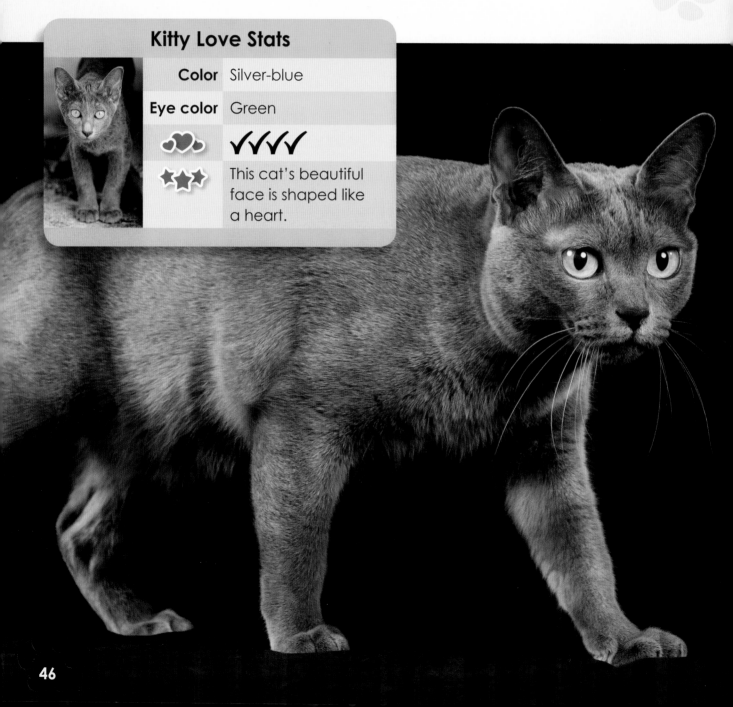

Kitty Love Stats

Color	Silver-blue
Eye color	Green

✓✓✓✓

This cat's beautiful face is shaped like a heart.

Gleaming silver-blue cats have been around for over 600 years. In Thailand the Korat is considered lucky. They were a popular present to a bride on her wedding day, always given in pairs.

Kurilian Bobtail

It looks robust, but this cat is sweet and gentle and just loves people.

Kitty Love Stats

Color	All colors
Eye color	All colors, including odd eyes
♥♥♥	✓✓✓✓✓
★★★	No two cats have exactly the same tail—each one is unique.

Cats with short tails have lived in the Kuril Islands—off the coast of Russia—for hundreds of years, but the breed is very rare. It makes a lovely family pet and will follow you around everywhere.

Maine Coon

This big cat is fluffy and friendly and just loves to be with you.

Kitty Love Stats

Color	All colors
Eye color	Blue, green, gold
🤍🤍	✓✓✓✓✓
⭐⭐	The Maine Coon will happily play "fetch" with you.

Maine Coons are the biggest of all the pet cat breeds, so it's a very good thing that they are so friendly. Maine Coons love people and they will follow you around like a dog. You can even teach them to walk on a leash.

Munchkin

This cutie is the "sausage dog" of the cat world. It's a little animal with a big personality.

Kitty Love Stats

Color	All colors
Eye color	All colors
♡♡	✓✓✓
⭐⭐	Munchkins love shiny things and will hide them to play with later.

Short-legged cats are often born naturally, but Munchkins have become so popular that they are now being bred specially—and it's easy to see why. Their little legs don't seem to stop them from loving life and all they want to do is play.

Nebelung

The German name, Nebelung, means "creature of the mist" because of the cat's silver-blue coat.

Kitty Love Stats

Color	Silver-blue
Eye color	Green
🤍🤍	✓✓✓✓✓
⭐⭐	This breed is shy and likes to sit up high and watch people.

A kitten named Siegfried started this lovely breed. He was the only blue longhaired kitten in a litter of four. The Nebelung has a mid-length, double coat that is blue underneath with silver tips, making it shimmer.

Norwegian Forest Cat

Friendly, fluffy, and gentle, this handsome cat will charm you.

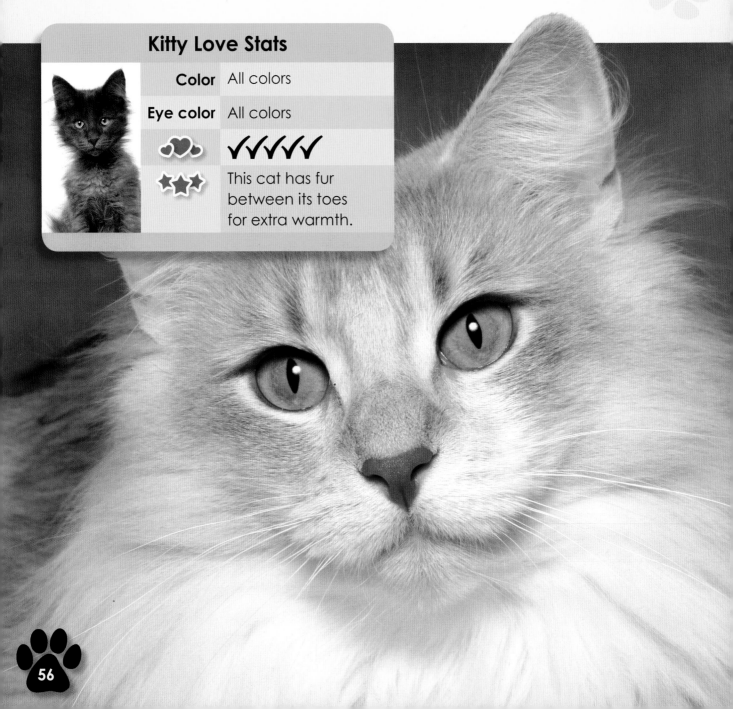

Kitty Love Stats

Color	All colors
Eye color	All colors
♥♥♥	✓✓✓✓✓
★★★	This cat has fur between its toes for extra warmth.

When the Vikings arrived in America more than a thousand years ago, they brought their cats with them. These animals had thick fur to survive cold northern winters and were very good at catching rats.

Ocicat

This cat got its name because it looks like an ocelot.

Kitty Love Stats

Color	Spotted
Eye color	All colors except blue
♡♡	✓✓✓
⭐⭐⭐	The first ever ocicat was a male named Tonga.

Despite its wild looks, the ocicat is very sweet natured and is not actually related to any wildcats. Instead it is the result of mixing Abyssinian, Siamese, and American Shorthair cats.

Oriental Shorthair

This strange-looking cat loves to be the center of attention.

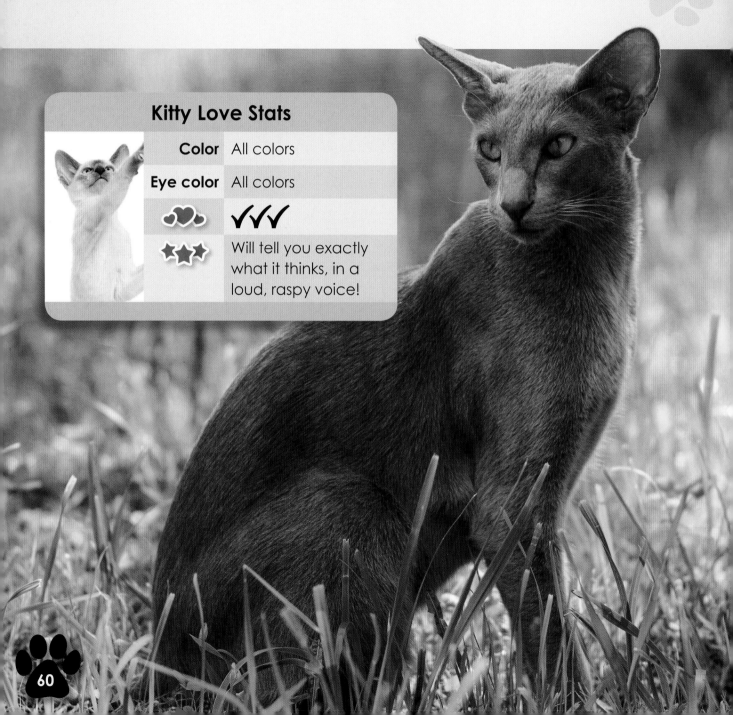

Kitty Love Stats

Color	All colors
Eye color	All colors
♥♥♥	✓✓✓
★★★	Will tell you exactly what it thinks, in a loud, raspy voice!

A mixture of Abyssinian, Siamese, and Russian Blue, this is possibly the smartest cat in the world. Your Oriental Shorthair will want lots of playtime with you—this is not a cat that is happy to be on its own.

Persian

This beautiful cat is one of the oldest breeds in the world.

Kitty Love Stats

Color	All colors	
Eye color	Copper, blue, green, odd	
🤍🤍	✓✓✓✓✓	
⭐⭐⭐	Quiet and sweet, the Persian is happiest sitting on your lap.	

Longhaired cats were thought to have come from Persia—now Iran—on the trade caravans that carried jewels and spices. The pretty Persian was loved by kings and queens.

Peterbald

This cat can be fuzzy like a peach or completely hairless.

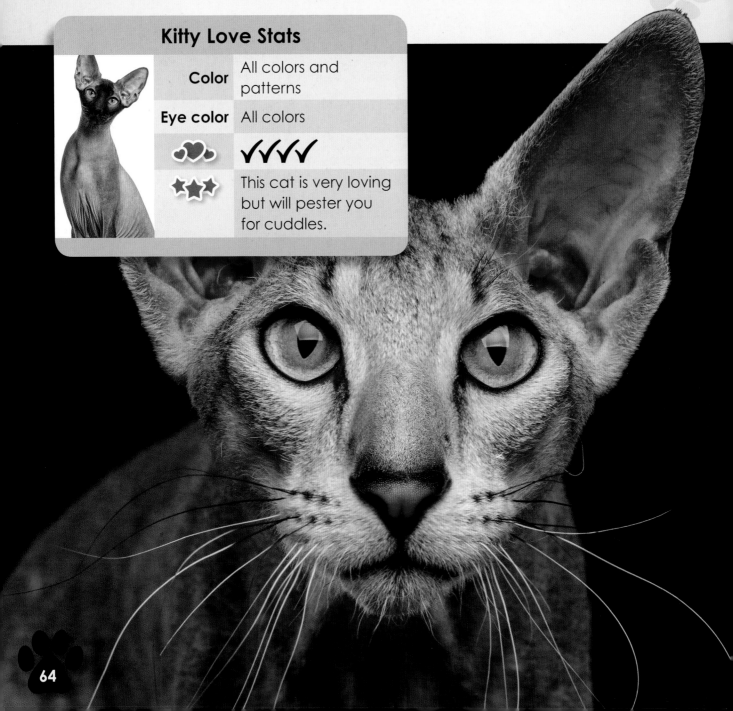

Kitty Love Stats

Color	All colors and patterns
Eye color	All colors
♥♥	✓✓✓✓
★★	This cat is very loving but will pester you for cuddles.

One of the newest cat breeds, the Peterbald comes from Russia. It has a unique coat; some have long fur that feels like soft velvet, and some have fur that feels like a man's bristly beard. Sometimes a Peterbald will have soft white patches and stubbly dark patches!

Ragamuffin

Like a puppy, this loving cat will follow you around.

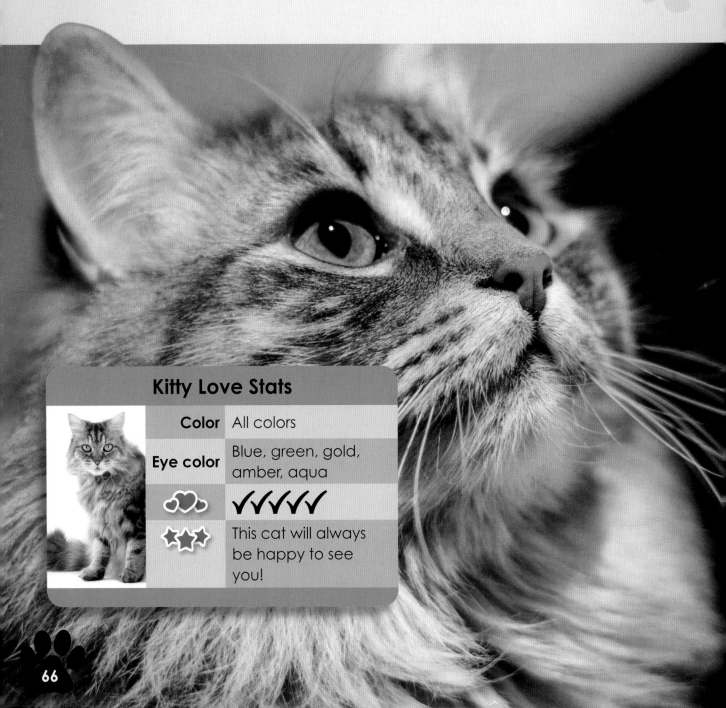

Kitty Love Stats

Color	All colors
Eye color	Blue, green, gold, amber, aqua
🤍🤍	✓✓✓✓✓
⭐⭐⭐	This cat will always be happy to see you!

The Ragamuffin is one of the prettiest and sweetest cats. It comes in all the colors you can imagine, and has the most fluffy tail. It is related to the Ragdoll and has many of its traits.

Ragdoll

This adorable cat will go limp in your arms like a doll.

Kitty Love Stats

Color	All colors
Eye color	Blue
♥♥	✓✓✓✓✓
⭐⭐⭐	Your cat will run to greet you at the door!

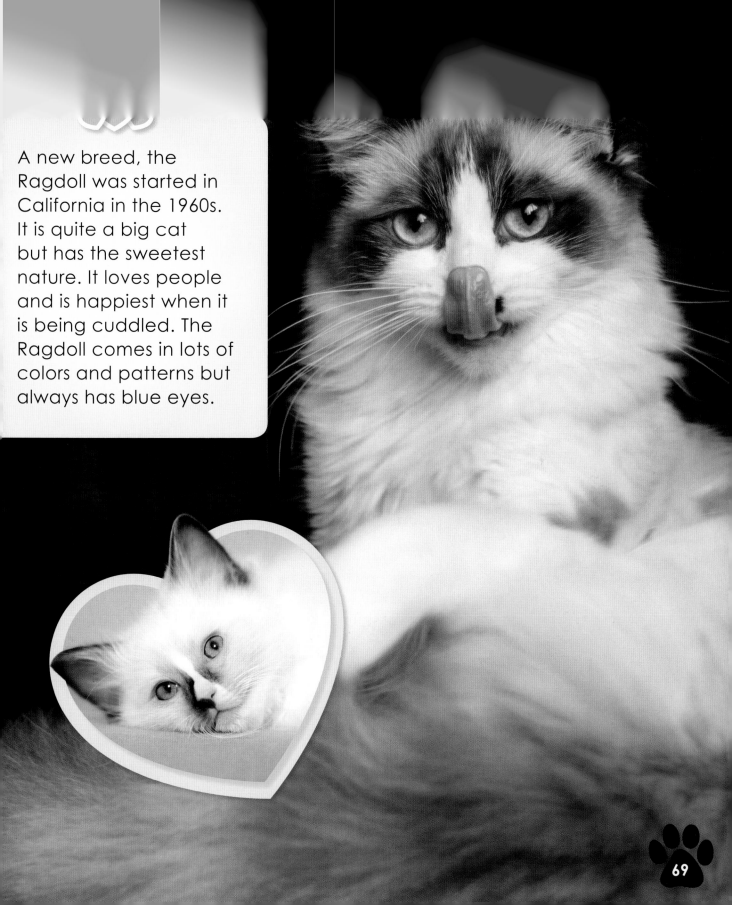

A new breed, the Ragdoll was started in California in the 1960s. It is quite a big cat but has the sweetest nature. It loves people and is happiest when it is being cuddled. The Ragdoll comes in lots of colors and patterns but always has blue eyes.

Russian Blue

That lovely silver-blue coat is as soft as silk.

Kitty Love Stats

Color	Blue
Eye color	Green
♥♥	✓✓✓✓
★★★	Its eyes turn a deeper green as it gets older.

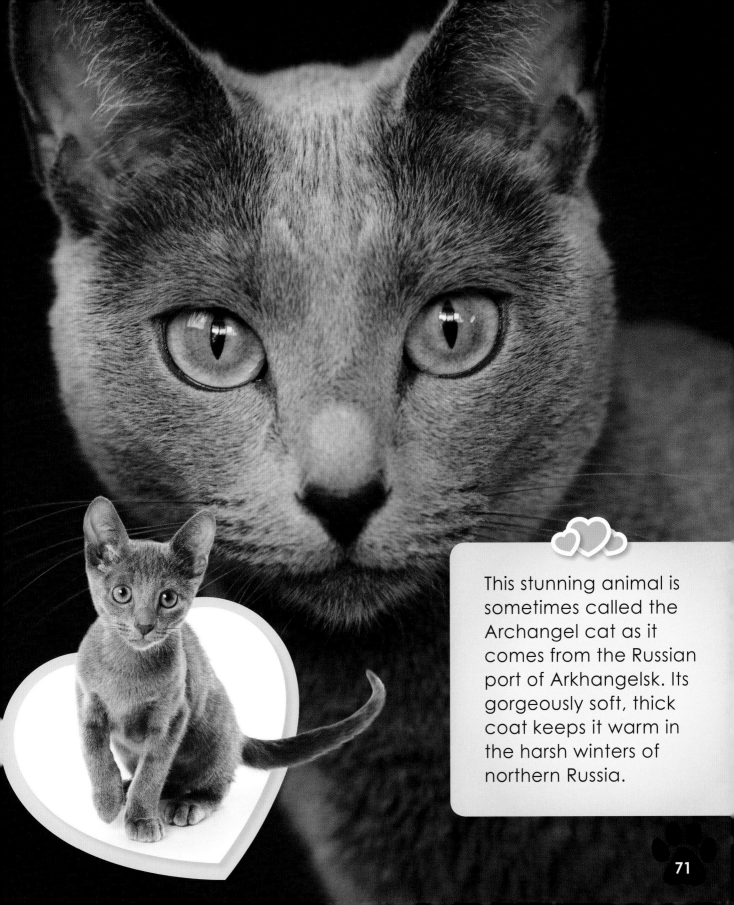

This stunning animal is sometimes called the Archangel cat as it comes from the Russian port of Arkhangelsk. Its gorgeously soft, thick coat keeps it warm in the harsh winters of northern Russia.

Savannah

The first cat of this kind was named Savannah —the striking breed was named after her.

Kitty Love Stats

Color	Brown, silver, black, smoke
Eye color	All colors
♡♡	✓✓✓
✦✦✦	Holds the world record for the tallest cat!

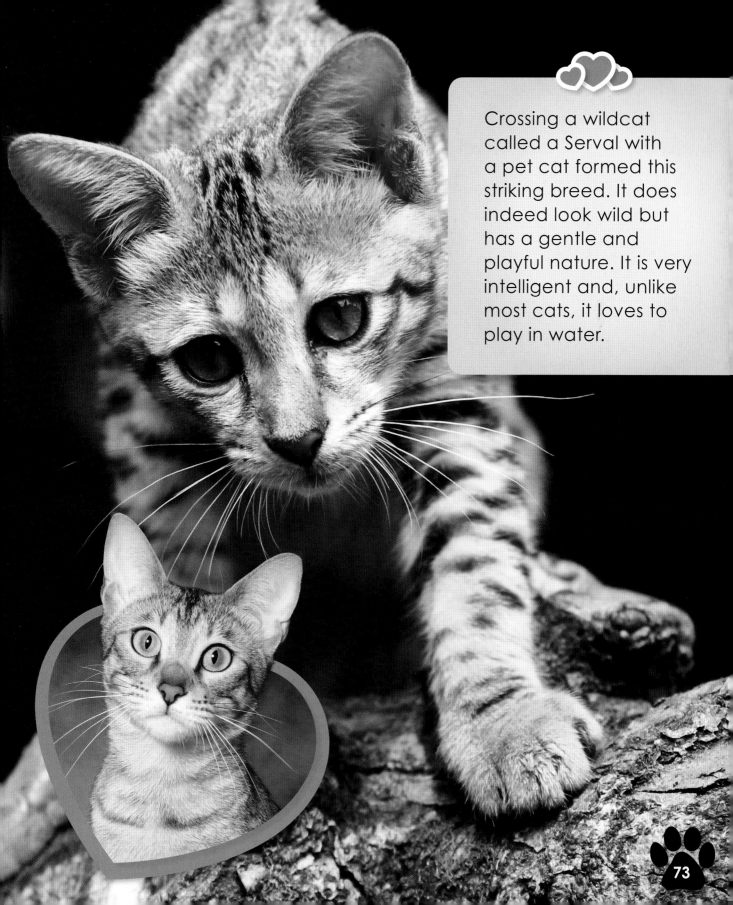

Crossing a wildcat called a Serval with a pet cat formed this striking breed. It does indeed look wild but has a gentle and playful nature. It is very intelligent and, unlike most cats, it loves to play in water.

73

Scottish Fold

Those cute folded ears set off its round face and round eyes.

Kitty Love Stats

Color	All colors	
Eye color	Mostly copper, but all colors	
🖤🖤🖤	✓✓✓✓✓	
⭐⭐⭐	Loves people and will follow you from room to room.	

All Scottish Folds can be traced back to a cat named Susie, who was born on a farm in Scotland in 1961. The kittens are born with straight ears, which fold over as they get older. They make calm and gentle pets.

Selkirk Rex

Like the other Rex cats, this breed has a soft and curly coat.

Kitty Love Stats

Color	All colors
Eye color	All colors
♥♥	✓✓✓✓✓
★★★	Sometimes called a "cat in sheep's clothing!"

Selkirk kittens can be born with straight and curly coats in the same litter. Some with straight fur will get curly later, but they will always have curly whiskers. This cat is loving and gentle so it makes a perfect family pet.

Siamese

Those dark ears, face, feet, and tail help to keep this cat cool.

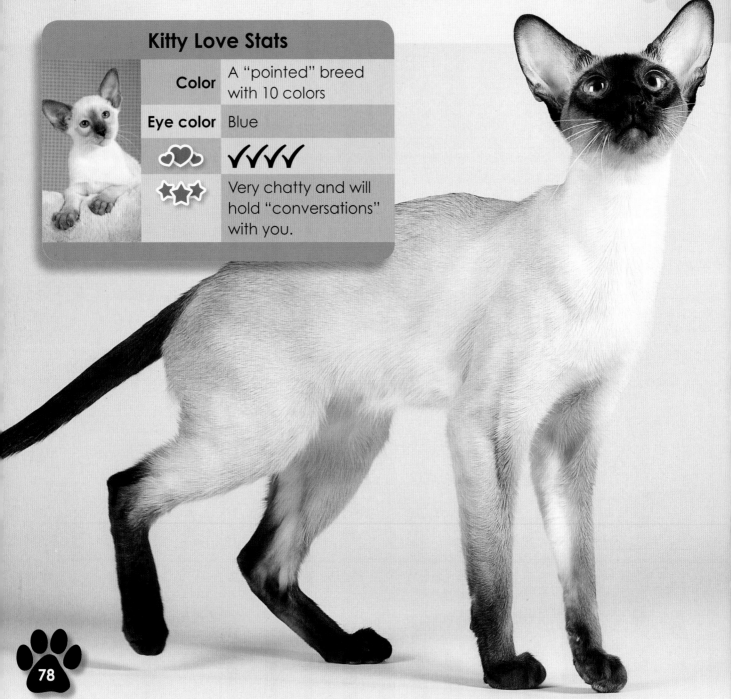

Kitty Love Stats

Color	A "pointed" breed with 10 colors
Eye color	Blue
♡♡♡	✓✓✓✓
★★★	Very chatty and will hold "conversations" with you.

An old breed, the Siamese is said to have the grace of a panther, the speed of a deer, the strength of a tiger, the loving nature of a dog, and the courage of a lion. It comes from Thailand, which was once called Siam.

Singapura

This cat was bred from four cats brought to America from Singapore.

Kitty Love Stats

Color	Brown and cream, with black markings
Eye color	Green, hazel, gold, copper
🖤🖤	✓✓✓✓✓
⭐⭐	This is the smallest of all cat breeds.

Don't be taken in by that clear-eyed little face. The Singapura is a bundle of mischief, always up to something. But you can never be cross with this cat because it has the sweetest, most loving nature.

Snowshoe

A pretty cat, this looks like a
Siamese but has white paws.

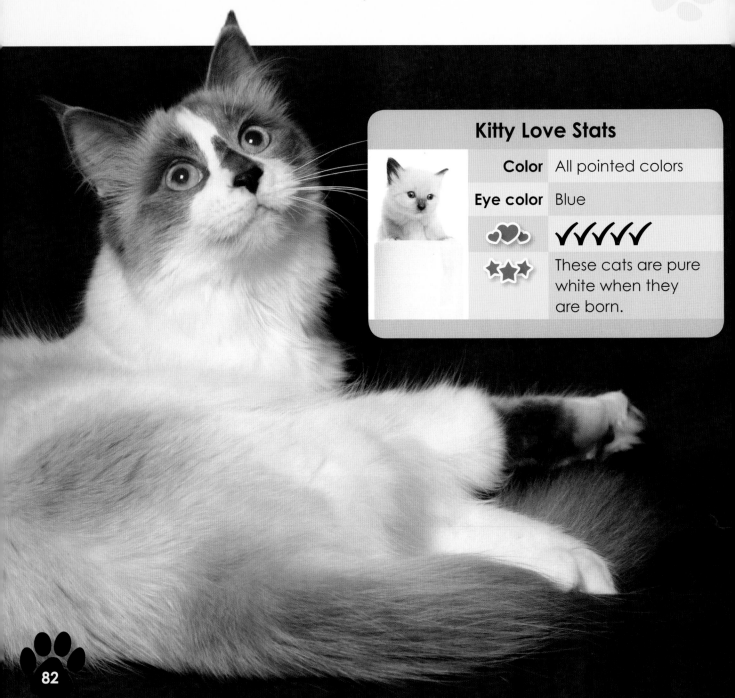

Kitty Love Stats

Color	All pointed colors
Eye color	Blue
♥♥♥	✓✓✓✓✓
★★★	These cats are pure white when they are born.

Every Snowshoe cat is unique, with distinct markings. It usually has a dark face with a V-shape from its eyes to its chin, dark ears and tail, and white feet. Its coat is soft and thick, and lovely to stroke.

83

Sokoke

In Kenya, people called this cat
kadzonzo, which means "like tree bark."

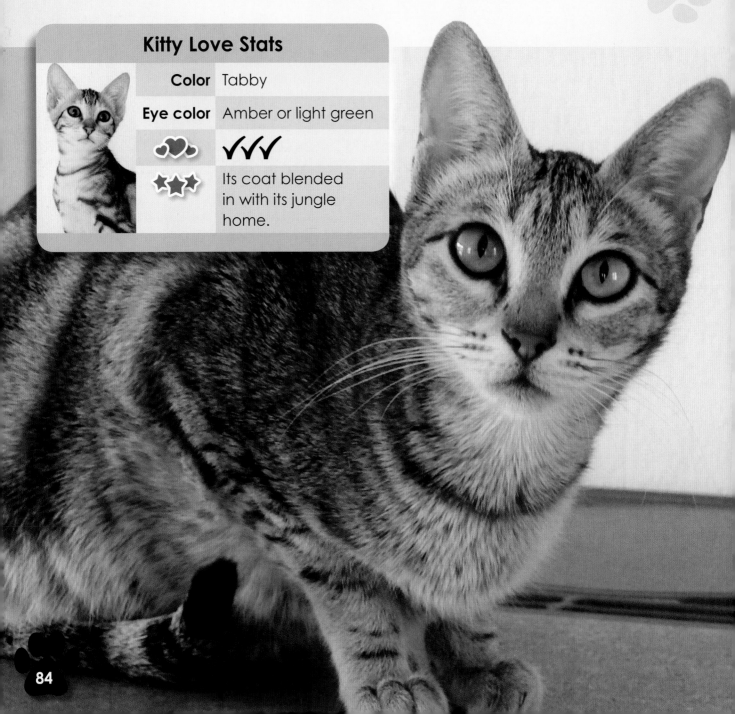

Kitty Love Stats

Color	Tabby
Eye color	Amber or light green
🖤🖤	✓✓✓
⭐⭐⭐	Its coat blended in with its jungle home.

This cat comes from the Arabuko Sokoke Forest in Kenya, Africa. Odd-looking kittens were found by a farmer and carefully bred to make the Sokoke. Though they look a little wild, they make happy pets.

Somali

With a fluffy ruff around its neck, this looks like a miniature lion!

Kitty Love Stats

Color	All colors, with ticking (small dark markings)
Eye color	Gold, green, hazel
☁☁	✓✓✓✓
★★★	This brainy cat loves to be the center of attention.

This cat is fairly new and is sometimes called a longhaired Abyssinian. It looks a little like the older Abyssinian breed, with the same attractive markings. Somalia is next to Ethiopia—once known as Abyssinia—on the African continent.

Sphynx

It might look bald, but this cat is covered with suede-like fuzz.

Kitty Love Stats

Color	All colors
Eye color	All colors
❤❤	✓✓✓✓
★★★	This cat doesn't have whiskers.

It shares its name with the Great Sphinx of Giza, an ancient statue in Egypt. Because the Sphynx feels the cold, some owners dress their pets in warm sweaters! But when you hold this cat, it will feel hot in your arms.

Tonkinese

A beautiful cat with "points" like a Siamese—but not so noisy!

Kitty Love Stats

Color	Solid, pointed, mink
Eye color	Aqua, blue, violet, yellow-green
♥♥	✓✓✓✓
★★	In 1970 a Tonkinese cat had 19 kittens!

Siamese and Burmese cats were used to make the Tonkinese. It is a very good-looking cat, with a sleek body, wedge-shaped head, and almond-shaped eyes. It has oval paws and is heavier to hold than it looks.

Turkish Angora

This old breed is thought to be related to the wild Manul cat of Asia.

Kitty Love Stats

Color	Mostly white
Eye color	Gold, green, blue, odd-eyed
🤍🤍	✓✓✓✓✓
⭐⭐	For many years, all longhaired cats were called Angoras.

This breed comes from the capital city of Turkey. It is known as the ballerina of the cat world for its grace. It is a pretty animal, with silky soft fur and a wide, sweet face.

93

Turkish Van

This cat loves to swim—and has a waterproof coat!

Kitty Love Stats

Color	White with colored patches
Eye color	Blue, amber, odd-eyed
🖤🖤🖤	✓✓✓✓✓
⭐⭐	In its home country, this cat is a national treasure.

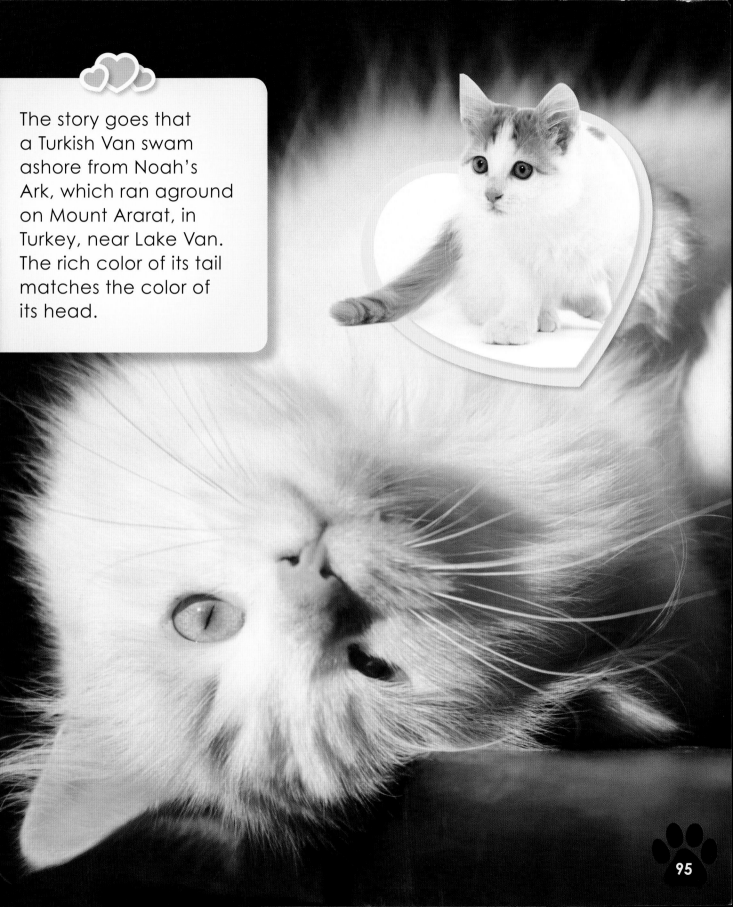

The story goes that a Turkish Van swam ashore from Noah's Ark, which ran aground on Mount Ararat, in Turkey, near Lake Van. The rich color of its tail matches the color of its head.

Picture acknowledgments

(t=top, b=bottom, l=left, r=right, fc=front cover, bc=back cover)

Alamy
1 Tierfotoagentur, 10bl Originoo Image Technologies Co. Limited, 12t Dorling Kindersley ltd, 12b JAV Clix / Stockimo, 13bl Dorling Kindersley ltd, 14tl Tierfotoagentur, 16b Sergey Taran, 17tr Zoonar GmbH, 17b blickwinkel, 19tl Juniors Bildarchiv GmbH, 22b Juniors Bildarchiv GmbH, 23l do_liux, 25l Juniors Bildarchiv GmbH, 26tr petographer, 28b Juniors Bildarchiv GmbH, 29b Juniors Bildarchiv GmbH, 31br Amy Lv, 34tl imageBROKER, 34b imageBROKER, 35br Dorling Kindersley ltd, 36b Arco Images GmbH, 41t Arco Images GmbH, 41b petographer, 42b Juniors Bildarchiv GmbH, 45br Juniors Bildarchiv GmbH, 49tr Tierfotoagentur, 53r Animal Photography, 54b Tierfotoagentur, 55l Tierfotoagentur, 55br imageBROKER, 56t Life on white, 56b Tierfotoagentur, 58t Tierfotoagentur, 61bl Tierfotoagentur, 62t LJ Wilson-Knight, 62b Photosforyou, 63r Juniors Bildarchiv GmbH, 64tl Life on white, 65tr Tierfotoagentur, 69l Tierfotoagentur, 70tl imageBROKER, 70b Tierfotoagentur, 71t Tierfotoagentur, 73t imageBROKER, 73bl Tierfotoagentur, 74t Juniors Bildarchiv GmbH, 75bl Natalya Onishchenko, 79br Arco Images GmbH, 80tl Tierfotoagentur, 80r Animal Photography, 82l Tierfotoagentur, 83l petographer, 83r Tierfotoagentur, 86l Tierfotoagentur, 86b David Kilpatrick, 87t David Kilpatrick, 87br Tierfotoagentur, 89br Animal Photography, 90l dezy, 91tl imageBROKER, 91b dezy, 92t Anastasia Koro, 93l MARKA, 94r Animal Photography, 95b Andrew Linscott, 96 Life on white

Dreamstime
31t © Li Cao

Edith Peulicke
84l, 84r

FLPA
33b Gerard Lacz, 39r J.-L. Klein and M.-L. Hubert, 45t J.-L. Klein and M.-L. Hubert, 58l Ramona Richter/Tierfotoagentur, 59t Ramona Richter/Tierfotoagentur, 81br Ramona Richter/Tierfotoagentur, 85r J.-L. Klein and M.-L. Hubert, 85bl J.-L. Klein and M.-L. Hubert, 90t Doreen Baum/Tierfotoagentur, 94t J.-L. Klein and M.-L. Hubert

Getty
40b Agency Animal Picture, 43t Steve Lupton, 57tr Ryuichi Miyazaki, 68b Rita Kapitulski, 69t Liz Wood Photography, 95tr Agency Animal Picture

Nature Picture Library
18b Mark Taylor, 92br © Klein & Hubert

Shutterstock
fc Alena Ozerova, bc vvvita, 2-3 alexavol, 4t JIHUN SHIN, 4b Kirill Vorobyev, 5t Kyselova Inna, 5br Anton Watman, 6r OrangeGroup, 6l cottonstudio, 7t Kucher Serhii, 7bl Konovalov Yevhenii, 8tl Eric Isselee, 8b janekub, 9 Eric Isselee, 9bl Robynrg, 10t Tony Campbell, 11tr Andrew Ivan, 11 Chendongshan, 13 OrangeGroup, 14 Rika-sama, 15tr Kucher Serhii, 15b Andrey_Kuzmin, 16tl Kirill Vorobyev, 19t Borkin Vadim, 19br Borkin Vadim, 20tr Eric Isselee, 20b Viktor Sergeevich, 21tl Andrey Kuzmichev, 21b Viktor Sergeevich, 22tl uzhursky, 23tr dezy, 24tr Jagodka, 24b Seregraff, 25r Jagodka, 26bl JE Jevgenija, 27t Zuzule, 27br JE Jevgenija, 28tl Eric Isselee, 29tr Eric Isselee, 30tr JAROON MAGNUCH, 30bl Kobpong Intawong, 32tl Natalia Fedosova, 32b Liliya Kulianionak, 33tl Okssi, 35t Pernille Westh, 36tl Ermolaev Alexander, 37tr Jagodka, 37b Seregraff, 38t hannadarzy, 38b kuban_girl, 39bl Sarah Fields Photography, 40tl izmargad, 42t Oliver Hoffmann, 43bl Eric Isselee, 44t Ekaterina Krivtsova, 44b dien, 46tl bonga1965,

46b BIGANDT.COM, 47tr Parichart Tungift, 47b Cyril PAPOT, 48t Nikolai Tsvetkov, 48b dien, 49l kuban_girl, 50t Happy monkey, 50b DenisNata, 51t otsphoto, 51bl Yury Barsukov, 52t SV_zt, 52b Shmeliova Natalia, 53l Phannasit, 54l Angel72, 57l Elisa Putti, 59bl dien, 60tl Eric Isselee, 60br Elena Masiutkina, 61l Bildagentur Zoonar GmbH, 63b Irina oxilixo Danilova, 64b Seregraff, 65b Toloubaev Stanislav, 66r Alex Papp, 66bl Scampi, 67r Evdoha_spb, 67l Tatiana Makotra, 68tl Linn Currie, 71b Utekhina Anna, 72tl alexavol, 72b Lindasj22, 74b vvvita, 75tr kuban_girl, 76t Eric Isselee, 76bl Jagodka, 77tr Jagodka, 77b Eric Isselee, 78tl Linn Currie, 78r vivver, 79t dedek, 81t Jenni Ferreira, 82tr Stephen Mcsweeny, 88l Seregraff, 88r Andrey_Kuzmin, 89t Eric Isselee, 93r Eric Isselee